TOO CUTE! BABY ANIMALS

Baby Foxes

by Colleen Sexton

Kaleidoscope
Minneapolis, MN

Where the Quest for Discovery Begins

This edition first published in 2024 by Kaleidoscope Publishing, Inc.
No part of this publication may be reproduced in whole or in part without written permission of the publisher.
For information regarding permission, write to

Kaleidoscope Publishing, Inc.
6012 Blue Circle Drive
Minnetonka, MN 55343

Library of Congress Control Number
2023936912

ISBN
978-1-64519-703-4 (library bound)
9-781-64519-751-5 (ebook)

Text copyright © 2024 by Kaleidoscope Publishing, Inc.
Bigfoot Books Jr. and associated logos are trademarks and/or registered trademarks of Kaleidoscope Publishing, Inc.

FIND ME IF YOU CAN!

Bigfoot Jr. lurks within one of the images in this book. It's up to you to find him!

Table of Contents

Hello, Pups! 4
From Head to Tail 10
On the Hunt 18
      Photo Glossary 22
      Read More 23
      Websites 23
      About the Author 24
      Index 24

Hello, Pups!

Baby foxes are born in a **den**.
They are called pups.

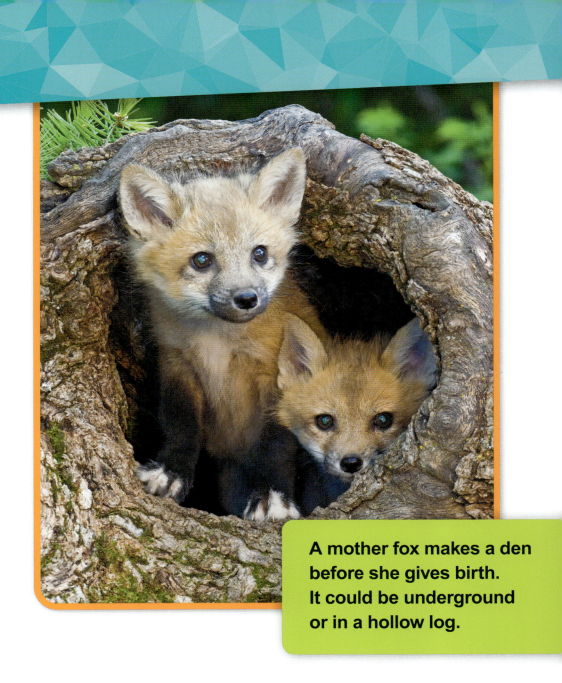

A mother fox makes a den before she gives birth. It could be underground or in a hollow log.

The pups make up a **litter**. A litter has many brothers and sisters.

The mother fox cares for the pups. She licks them clean and keeps them warm.

Pups drink milk for about three weeks. Then their mother also feeds them pieces of meat.

The pups drink milk from their mother's body.

The father fox goes hunting. He brings back meat for his family.

FUN FACT
Male foxes are called dogs. Female foxes are called vixens.

YAWN! The pups curl up together to sleep.

Fox pups sleep about 20 hours a day.

From Head to Tail

One day, a pup wiggles its narrow body out of the den. Fluffy fur keeps it warm in the cool air.

The pup runs and jumps on long legs. It wags its furry tail.

young red fox

adult red fox

A fox pup's fur changes color as it grows up.

The pup stands on padded paws. Each paw has four toes. Each front paw also has a **dewclaw**.

The pup tilts its round head. It **twitches** the nose at the end of its long **snout**.

FUN FACT
Foxes sweat through their paws and pant to cool down.

FUN FACT

Fox pups are born with blue eyes. Their eyes turn yellow as they grow up.

The pup's large eyes help it see well at night.

The pup hears a noise. It turns its pointed ears in the direction of the sound.

A fox can hear a mouse squeak from 100 feet (30 meters) away. That's about the length of a basketball court!

Fox Facts

Kind of Animal: mammal

Size at Birth: about the size of a pear

Litter Size: about three to nine pups

Home: farmland, forests, grasslands, cities

On the Hunt

The pups learn hunting skills. They chase each other. They **pounce** on sticks and leaves.

FUN FACT
Some foxes hunt where people live. They push over garbage cans to find food.

One night, the pups go on a hunt. Their mother puts her nose to the ground. She picks up the smell of a mouse.

The pups watch as their mother quietly creeps toward the mouse. Then she pounces!

Soon the hunt is on again. The pups follow their mother in search of more **prey**.

What Do Foxes Eat?

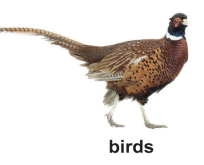
birds

rabbits

squirrels

mice

frogs

berries

FUN FACT
A pup leaves to live and hunt on its own when it is about six months old.

Photo Glossary

den: a place where an animal lives and gives birth

dewclaw: a toe and claw that is higher up than the rest of the toes; the dewclaws do not touch the ground when a fox walks.

litter: a group of babies born at one time

mammal: a warm-blooded animal that has hair or fur; mammals drink their mother's milk.

pant: to breathe quickly

pounce: to jump on something suddenly

prey: animals that are hunted by other animals for food

snout: the long nose and jaws of an animal

twitches: quickly moves back and forth

Read More

Myers, Maya. *Little Kids First Big Book of Baby Animals.* Washington, D.C.: National Geographic Kids, 2022.

Perish, Patrick. *Red Foxes.* Minneapolis, Minn.: Bellwether Media, 2022.

Ruby, Rex. *Inside a Fox's Den.* Minneapolis, Minn.: Bearport Publishing, 2023.

Websites

Factsurfer.com gives you a safe, fun way to find more information.

1. Go to www.factsurfer.com.
2. Enter "Baby Foxes" into the search box and click 🔍
3. Select your book cover to see a list of related websites.

About the Author

Colleen Sexton is a writer and editor. She is the author of more than 100 nonfiction books for kids on topics ranging from astronauts to glaciers to elephants. She lives in Minnesota.

INDEX

den 4, 5, 10
father 8
fur 10, 11
hunt 8, 18, 19, 20, 21
litter 5, 17
mother 5, 6, 7, 19, 20
pounce 18, 20
sleep 9

PHOTO CREDITS

The images in this book are reproduced through the courtesy of: Pim Leijen/Shutterstock Images, cover; KJ Quraish/Shutterstock Images, title page, 17; Eric Isselee/Shutterstock Images, p. 3; Miroslav Hlavko/Shutterstock Images, p. 4; Jack Nevitt/Shutterstock Images, p. 5; Menno Schaefer/Shutterstock Images, p. 6; Ghost Bear/Shutterstock Images, p. 7; Menno Schaefer/Shutterstock Images, p. 8; Menno Schaefer/Shutterstock Images, p. 9 (top); Africa Studio/Shutterstock Images, p. 9 (bottom); Harry Collins Photography/Shutterstock Images, p. 10; WildlifeWorld/Shutterstock Images, p. 11 (top); slowmotiongli/Shutterstock Images, p. 11 (bottom left)); Rejean Aline Bedard/Shutterstock Images, p. 11 (bottom right); Dee Carpenter Originals/Shutterstock Images, p. 12; Oleksandr Lytvynenko/Shutterstock Images, p. 13; WildlifeWorld/Shutterstock Images, p. 14; slowmotiongli/Shutterstock Images, p. 15; Oleksandr Lytvynenko/Shutterstock Images, p. 16; Menno Schaefer/Shutterstock Images, p. 18; Rostislav Stach/Shutterstock Images, p. 19; David OBrien/Shutterstock Images, p. 20; gowithstock/Shutterstock Images, p. 21 (berries); photomaster/Shutterstock Images, p. 21 (birds); Eric Isselee/Shutterstock Images, p. 21 (frogs); Egoreichenkov Evgenii/Shutterstock Images, p. 21 (mice); Elena Elisseeva/Shutterstock Images, p. 21 (rabbits); Bob Deering/Shutterstock Images, p. 21 (squirrels); Menno Schaefer/Shutterstock Images, p. 21 (bottom); Mia Woolgar/Shutterstock Images, p. 22 (den); Richard Peterson/Shutterstock Images, p. 22, 23 (dewclaw); Miroslav Hlavko/Shutterstock Images, p. 22 (litter); BlueBarronPhoto/Shutterstock Images, p. 22 (mammal); slowmotiongli/Shutterstock Images, p. 22 (pant); Stanislav Duben/Shutterstock Images, p. 22 (pounce); Menno Schaefer/Shutterstock Images, p. 22 (prey); Menno Schaefer/Shutterstock Images, p. 22 (snout); Oleksandr Lytvynenko/Shutterstock Images, p. 22 (twitches).